Also by Tarra Judson Stariell

*Sanity Lost and Found:
A True Story of Brainwashing and Recovery*

FLASHPOINTS of AWARENESS

Lessons Learned from a Life

TARRA JUDSON STARIELL

Flashpoints of Awareness: Lessons Learned from a Life
Copyright © 2023 by Tarra Judson Stariell
Published in the United States of America by Ranch House Press.

All rights reserved. No part of this book may be used or reproduced in any manner whatsoever without written permission except in the case of brief quotations embodied in critical articles and reviews. For information contact:
Ranch House Press
PO Box 241
Escondido, CA 92033

Illustrations by Joel Paola
Cover and interior design by GKS Creative, Nashville, TN.

Library of Congress Cataloging-in-Publication Data has been applied for.

ISBN 978-0-9992955-3-3 Paperback
ISBN 978-0-9992955-4-0 eBook

Printed in the United States of America

This book is dedicated to all of you beautiful souls in this world. May you discover the light within your being and allow yourselves to be gently guided by your right-mind in discovering the love, peace, joy, well-being, and peace of mind awaiting you.

Contents

Preface 1

Mona 9

The Hay Hook 13

Maverick 19

Plywood Miracle 23

Winged Brethren 25

Am I Loveable? 27

Leaving San Pasqual 31

Ma'am 41

Pause for Reflection 45

The Camino 49

Eddie 61

Another Transition 67

Exercises for Self-Regulation and Forgiveness 73

Acknowledgements 81

About the Author 85

Preface

THANK YOU for your interest in reading these true stories. Like using GPS when finding our way to a destination, the Holy Spirit, the spark of divinity that we each have within our minds, has assisted me through these pratfalls and challenges. I am extremely grateful for all the help I have received. When practicing as a psychotherapist, I made a promise to my clients not to write about their experiences and instead am sharing some of the lessons I have learned. My hope is that they will serve you in some way, and perhaps contribute to your well-being and spiritual awareness.

In the early 1970s, I absolutely loved my work with the Peace Corps, Colombia. So much, that I had planned on spending several more years in Colombia and afterwards, traveling the world. My quest was in search of answers to explain why there was so much suffering like the poverty I was working to correct. That is, until one night when I witnessed the formation of two inexplicable electric bluish-white lights take shape to my left. From these two rays, the following words flooded into my mind: "Life as you know it on planet earth will not continue to be the same unless humans change the way that they are living." I subsequently heard that I should return to the States and spread this message. Despite my immediate protests, numerous images appeared in my mind's eye, reminiscent of what we now see world-wide with the influences of global warming.

Reluctantly, I ended my time with the Peace Corps, returned to my roots and began my attempts to translate what I had experienced. As I searched for an effective way to share the message given me, I floundered in various jobs and disciplines and even dove into several self-help movements. Thinking I could bring more awareness to people about the earth, plant, and animal species sharing it with us, I formed my own landscaping and gardening business called The Earth Works.

My journey from a troubled childhood to my time in the Peace Corps, more than twelve years in a cult and my subsequent recovery and becoming a therapist myself, is all chronicled in my first book, *Sanity Lost and Found: A True Story of Brainwashing and Recovery*.

I do not celebrate that what was told to me seems like it is becoming a reality. Nor do I recommend dedicating one's life to saving the world or, let alone, entering a cult. However, I am grateful for all of my experiences, no matter how painful they seemed at the time, for they have led me to seek even deeper answers to the enigma of life.

Through my efforts to "save the world," I came to recognize that the world does not need saving. Rather, we do. It would seem that in our lives today, many of us are like the prisoners of Plato's Cave in that we have mistaken appearances for reality and live accordingly within that belief system. We seem too often to be conducting our lives as if we are separate individuals, independent from the effects of our thoughts and behaviors on ourselves as well as others. Albert Einstein thought otherwise and stated the following: "A person experiences life as something separated from the rest—a kind of optical delusion of consciousness. Our task must be to free ourselves from this self-imposed prison, and through compassion, to find the reality of Oneness."

During my recovery, I lived with my beloved grandmother on the family's former ranch, our childhood refuge. While attending graduate school and turning my life around, arc welding became a passion of mine. Much of the ranch had stood still for almost twenty years after the cows were sold. My father had arranged for his workers to find jobs elsewhere, sold much of the working machinery but kept a Bobcat and a Ford 4n skip loader.

The dairy had occupied the same land for over a hundred years and above the hay barns and away from everything was a graveyard of abandoned farm equipment. Horse drawn plows, wagons, and others, stood rusting beside tractor driven bailers, manure spreaders, sickle bar mowers, discs, and the like. All had been left as newer models replaced them.

Using an arc welder and acetylene torch, I happily repurposed them for my outsider art. For my "shopping trips," I would drive the 4n skip loader to this graveyard of possibilities to survey these relics. As each one called to me, I piled them into the bucket of the tractor and proceeded back to my workshop.

When iron is heated to a liquid viscosity it is then available to meld with another substance. Thus, the phenomenon of "welding" two objects together. That moment of viscosity between these previously three-dimensional "hard as steel" objects is the "flashpoint." The experience was thrilling as I witnessed the suspension of physical laws for another possibility.

To me, jumping dimensions seems to be what we humans are capable of when we open our minds to another way of living. That would be "right-minded thinking" (being mindful) or recognizing that we (all races, cultures, genders, religions, sexual orientations, plants, animals, et cetera—you get the picture) are not separate but rather joined in shared interests. Furthermore, perhaps we might also recognize we are all siblings living on the same global home, rather than the wrong-minded (mindless, ego driven, judgmental) thinking that we are separate, and that some are worthier than others. Surrendering our ego to the Spirit within us is what I liken to being guided by our right-mind. Our brains and bodies will manifest whichever messages are sent from our minds, whether from our "ego mind" or our Spirit informed "right mind."

I believe that despite the chaos in the world, all is not lost for we are also witnessing and benefiting from many relatively recent discoveries. I will limit this to a brief discussion of what quantum physics and psychology have brought to our awareness. Because of our growing knowledge of quantum physics, we now have lasers, fax machines, cell phones, medical imaging and the like. All from previously unknown properties and capabilities within our phenomenal world. Additionally, it has given us such aphorisms as "what you resist, persists," or simply put, resistance causes persistence. "Energy follows focus" is another among the many. Some ancient spiritual texts are permeated with similar concepts like "what goes around, comes around." For some, it has taken modern science to validate and accept this as a reality.

Fairly recently, quantum scientists have presented the "holographic universe philosophy" that states we are living in an illusion as projected images from elsewhere. Leonard Susskind discovered the mathematical equation proving such.

In the realm of understanding human behavior, Freud, most notably, contributed to our knowledge about the defense mechanisms humans utilize in avoidance of reality. Denial, repression, and projection foster the continued misperceptions and subsequent suffering that we humans endure. This belief system also gives rise to another that we are separate entities with separate interests.

Denial is a form of judgment because it does not allow acceptance of "what is." Denial causes repression, a stuffing away of present reality, usually a negative experience, emotional reactions, negative cognitions, and/or bodily sensations related to a specific event or events. Hastily moving away from accepting the discomfort and need for correction of a situation, our "defenses" allow us to push it aside in the fantasy that we no longer have to deal with it. However, what is repressed is suppressed or stored in our unconscious mind. Additionally, what is suppressed, will either return to the body or be projected outward and thus manifested in the behavior of another or an object in our external environment. This phenomenon ensures that our failed lessons and poor choices return to us to be learned and therefore corrected. Denying the lessons in front of us ensures our continual existence in a dissociated reality; doomed to the hamster wheel of seeking, but never finding, peace of mind. However, like gravity, the truth will always return to us to be once again rejected or acknowledged. Each time, the consequences growing more dire until we leave Plato's Cave of our darkened and distorted awareness.

Through these stories you will witness my experiential journey with ineffective defense mechanisms and the discovery and employment of successful alternatives for coping with life's vicissitudes. They have been, along with the rest of my life, my learning curriculum. When my normal way of ego-minded thinking was suspended, a new and more enlightened awareness flooded into my mind. Life is so much easier, enjoyable, loving, and peaceful when I remember these lessons. I therefore am sharing them in hopes of the same for you.

Mona

Bright, shiny faces surrounded me in the hot tropical sun, moving closer to examine this strange one in their midst. Crushing in on me, needing to be touched, held, and hugged, I gathered their small bodies in my arms, as many as I could hug until the next wave crowded in. I was their "Sen'or," a slang term they used for a woman of authority, working with one of the nuns at the daycare center for these former latchkey children of the ghetto.

Flashpoints of Awareness

Victims of forced relocation, their mothers were in the "centro" (center of town) washing clothes all day for the pittance they would bring home. These families had been forced from their homes, "tugurios" (slums) of stilted wooden huts on the waterfront with life-sustaining access to the ocean. Representing an embarrassment and ugly reality to tourists traveling from the airport in Crespo to the mecca of high-rise hotels and elegant restaurants in Boca Grande, the tugurios were razed and their inhabitants forced elsewhere. Relegated to square homes on the clay-filled slopes towering above the city, the journey for food and work had become an hour's bus ride or more.

Sole providers, these mothers with few choices, left their children in darkened huts with dirt floors and scant to eat. In the early 1970s, the newly formed Colombian social services agency and the Peace Corps were working to rescue these children from malnutrition and starvation. With bellies filled with food provided by the Care Program, they could now reclaim the playfulness and desire for learning of youth.

At ease with their new-found familiarity, I felt a mild tugging on my legs, drawing attention to the many dark hands extending blond leg hairs out for examination. "Mona" (cute) they delightedly giggled. "Mona," they repeated with more giggles, surprised that a woman could possess such blond hairs on her legs like the monkeys in their open market. Their wide-eyed wonder touched me deeply as they accepted my diversity without fear or judgment.

What a wonderful world we would live in if we could allow the differences among us to be accepted with open hearts and minds free of judgment.

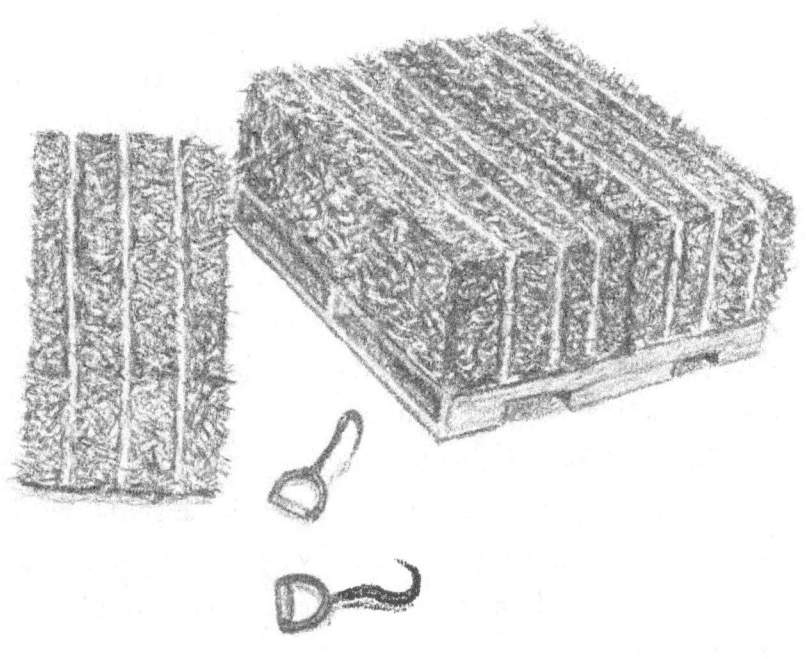

The Hay Hook

Rushing up to the barn, with no time to feed the horses, I was going to be late for school, an hour's drive away.

"*Why do you do this to yourself? You're always late, trying to accomplish too many things at once*" my mind railed at me as I approached where we kept the hay.

"Dammit! Why can't people stack the hay on top of the pallet where it belongs? It will get moldy lying here on the cement!"

Now even more ungrounded with anger, I grabbed a hay hook in each hand and swung them into the sides of the bale of hay to lift it onto the pallet. "Bing," the right one bounced off the bale and found a grab hole in my knee.

"OW!!! OH MY GOD!!! OW, OW!!!"

Howling with pain, I fell backward onto the bale and pulled the hook from my knee. Cradling it, I rocked back and forth and cried silently with the pain.

"Ow! Ow! Ow! Oh, that hurts!"

I indulged in my self-pity until realizing it was getting even later. Staggering to my feet, I carefully sank a hook into each side and lifted the bale onto the pallet so I could open it and feed the horses.

"For sure I'm going to be late now. Why do these things happen to me?"

Hobbling back to the horse pasture with flakes of hay, I remembered, *"what goes around, comes around."*

"Oh fine. So, I'm responsible for hurting myself because I was angry about always being late. Well, if the bale had been put where it belonged, maybe I would not have hurt myself," I justified.

Driving to school, the battle inside my head continued. *"Okay, so I've been angry at myself for all my failures. Can't I even be angry for being a victim of my circumstances?"* I argued with a more rational side of my mind, trying to present another option to me.

"I know that blaming my parents doesn't help . . . And staying angry at the cult leader is like eating poison. Arghhh! I suppose he was doing the best that he could, but it still wasn't right! God, I'm still so angry at him!"

School was helping to put the pieces together of how I had become so vulnerable to being brainwashed and subsequently abused. However, the more I thrashed about looking for reasons, the more I judged myself for my past errors and lack of discernment. In turn, more physical calamities befell my person. *"Surely, someone is to blame for all this!"*

Freud and his discoveries were a topic in class one day. He introduced the phenomenon called "Psychological Projection." It is a defense mechanism that humans do when they resist taking responsibility for their thoughts, feelings, and behaviors—whether for reasons conscious or unconscious to them. Like a movie being projected onto the screen, people, places, or things become the object upon which we "project" blame, guilt, and shame onto others for what we do not want to recognize is in ourselves. I had yet to realize that no conscious adult can be forced by someone to feel or do something against their will.

Rather, my anger kept me focused on finding someone or something to blame for my upsets and failures. I was engaged in a seemingly endless cycle of harboring negative emotions and then getting upset with their consequences to my life or body, fueling more upsets as the cycle continued. This drama served to dissociate me farther from recognizing these cycles and their consequences and the alternative to these habituated reactions. I had yet to learn how to consistently explore what I was experiencing, feel my emotions, forgive, and neutralize them without projecting or acting on them.

Months later, while getting ready to ride my horse with a friend, she shared hurt feelings about something I had done involving her. "Didn't you realize how painful that was for me?"

"No, I obviously didn't. I was so overwhelmed with grieving my father's death and all the familial trauma drama that went with it. I never meant to hurt you but can see that I did. I'm truly sorry."

Feeling incredibly ashamed for how I had behaved with a dear and valued friend, I quickly finished saddling my horse and rode ahead, wanting to get away from her and facing the pain I had caused.

"How could I have done that? And how could I have been so mindless? What was I thinking? Why was I so blind and not seeing what I was doing?"

With each step my horse took I was disliking myself even more as I mulled this over. Lost in this shame spiral, I was far down the rabbit hole when a cat ran out from the brush, right in front of my horse.

The Hay Hook

Immediately spinning around in the opposite direction, he bolted into a gallop and my saddle with me in it, slipped over to one side. *"Got to grab the reins."*

"Whoa, Cash. Slow down, boy." He was at a full gallop now, and I was still grappling for the reins when I spied a rock jutting up in the path as my horse sped on. *"My head's going to hit that rock. Get off!"*

Lying on the ground, I was hurting with embarrassment now added to my shame. Cash came up to me, having stopped and turned around as soon as I fell off.

"Hey, boy. Thanks for stopping now but that was only a cat."

"Tarra, are you okay?" my friend asked, approaching me after dismounting.

"Not really. I just need to lie here for a few minutes and gather my thoughts."

"Oh, that hurts. Man, I was really beating myself up right before that happened. I feel so ashamed but truly didn't mean to hurt her. Why did that happen? It seems like every time I hate myself, I get hurt."

"Do you think you can ever forgive me for what I did? I am so sorry."

"Of course, Tarra. I know you didn't do it on purpose, but I wanted you to know how much that hurt me in hopes you wouldn't do it again. I forgive you."

Breathing out a sigh of relief, with tears welling up I almost whispered, "Thank you!" Getting back on my feet, I added, "Thank you! I think I just learned some incredible lessons about myself. I'm truly sorry and thank you again for telling me."

I tightened the cinch I had neglected to reinforce after saddling my horse. Distancing myself from reality and the shame I had felt, I forgot to remedy how my horse would bloat himself to keep the cinch loose. Mounting him again, we continued our ride, this time enjoying myself without the burden of all my self-loathing.

Maverick

Living in the back country offers a different perspective on the survival of animals. Somehow, too many folks have believed the dogs or cats they dropped off would be able to fend for themselves. Most did not survive. However, Amadeus and then Maverick were two abandoned cats who had managed to evade the ever-present coyotes enjoying a regular menu of stray cats.

After returning from school and work one day, a very large yellow cat followed me to the house from my makeshift garage, formerly a calf pen. I easily relented and gave him some loving, after he howled the entire time. I also started leaving food for him on one of the rafters of the ranch work sheds that were open and a safe haven for such felines.

"Amadeus," a Maine Coon, became a welcome addition to our household but remained outside until one night when he managed to break into an upstairs window and into our hearts. Taking him to the vet, Amadeus was tested, neutered, vaccinated, and then adopted into our household. He was given free rein to roam outside until dark.

Over time, several other cats wandered into the yard but did not linger or return, no doubt becoming coyote food. Maverick, the other exception, was an orange tabby, but smaller than Amadeus. Offering him food, I attempted to approach him. Away he went, so I left the food under a tree and backed off. Watching him return, he bolted down his food, and quickly disappeared.

As time passed, Maverick let me pet and then pick him up. Stiff as a board at first, he trembled as I held and stroked him, speaking softly as I did. Eventually, his trauma eased enough to visit the vet for his makeover.

"Someone has been very cruel to this cat. He has a heart murmur, maybe from someone kicking him. He probably will not have a long life. So sad." She shared after examining him before all his procedures.

The "boys" lived well together until late one night, I heard a scream from Maverick. Rushing over to him, he was still crying in pain and could not move his hind legs.

"Oh, buddy. I'm so sorry!"

I gently wrapped him in a towel, and we rushed to the emergency animal clinic. His cries grew softer as I tried soothing him with voice and touch.

"May I help you?" I was asked as we entered the clinic.

"Yes, my cat has lost the use of his hind legs and I'd like you to help ease his pain."

"We need to see some form of payment first."

I fumbled through my purse to find a credit card. "Here."

"Okay. The doctor will be out shortly to examine him to see how we can help him."

"His vet said he has a heart murmur and I know he's hurting right now. Could you please give him something for his pain. I don't think there's any coming back from this and I don't want him to suffer."

"All right, I'll get the vet right now."

"Thank you!"

A white coat approached us, holding a syringe. He briefly examined Maverick and offered his opinion. "It is evident that his hind legs are paralyzed. I'm sorry. This should calm him."

The vet worked deftly as he spoke, and Maverick stopped crying as his body relaxed a little in my arms.

"I just gave him a sedative to ease his pain, but he should probably be euthanized."

"Yes, I know. Please give me a minute with him. I'd also like to hold him while you put him to sleep if that's okay."

"Sure, I understand."

As they prepped his leg for the fatal IV, I started crying.

"Are you ready?"

I nodded.

Through my tears, I could feel Maverick's heart beating as I held him and then suddenly it stopped. At that moment, my heart filled with the most incredible love and joyous sensation. At first, I did not understand what this was.

"Maverick, you're free! You're no longer in pain and yet you're still alive! Huh! What an incredible gift you've given me, letting me know you've crossed over and yet still exist. Thank you! I love you, Maverick, and will miss you very much."

Plywood Miracle

In 2007, there were 1200 of us who lost our homes when the Witch Creek Fire raged through the backcountry where I lived. At the time, our collective loss was monumental. Alas, not so since then.

Despite feeling empty and despondent, I had successfully extinguished the recurring voice of shame within me, asking, "Why didn't you take that?" and so on, when I recalled lost possessions. I was also grieving the loss of many other lives. I had been nurturing over 120 macadamia, avocado, and fruit trees, and the surrounding wildlife.

Returning to my property, I roamed the charred remains and ash from another time. Memories of the abundant vegetation and wildlife before the fire challenged me inordinately.

"I know that fire is a part of nature, which can be cruel, but I wish I didn't have to witness all this devastation."

As I stumbled along, kicking up clouds of ash with each step, I came upon a piece of partially burned plywood that had blown off the stack I had, at least 500 yards away. Curious, I lifted one corner and hovering underneath was a lizard. Dropping to my knees, I cried in gratitude to see this testament to resilience, surviving by taking refuge under the plywood. I had never felt so deeply for a simple lizard.

"I wish it hadn't taken such extreme circumstances to humble me into respecting another form of life that I normally ignore."

Winged Brethren

One day while driving back with a friend after horseback riding, I noticed a hawk squatting on the road ahead. "Slow down!" I blurted out to the car in front of us as I watched the bird take flight.

Without hesitating, the car sped on, hitting the raptor and sending it hurtling to the side of the road.

"Please stop the car," I urged my friend and ran to the bird, lying on its back. "*Is it alive?*" I wondered to myself. As I was standing there, the bird suddenly righted itself. Shaking its head from side to side, its eyes slowly drifted into focus.

"Are you okay?" I asked, not thinking about talking to a wild bird. It eyeballed me during a very long silence, and then with a leap and flapping of wings, the bird soared high above and away from the oncoming traffic.

"Wow! That felt great!"

The love I have for nature is not blind; nature can be cruel as are we when we don't use our right minds. But this time, a wild creature lived to soar through another day.

Walking back to the car, I mused out loud, "Maybe he just needed a loving connection to awaken."

Am I Loveable?

As I mentioned earlier, my adobe home did not survive one of the first major firestorms to blaze through California. It was the largest then but has since been dwarfed by ever more massive wildfires throughout the world, testimonies to our warming planet with climate change. The current flood of rain and snow has given rise to a wondrous rebirth of vegetation, leaving one to question what is next in this global weather-lottery.

I spent many blessed years with my dear grandmother before moving into my own home after she had passed away. I was able to enjoy mine for a year before it was leveled to dust and ash. In that fire I also witnessed family homes and ranches, dating back to 1882, go up in smoke.

The shock of my loss seemed absolute and had loosened an old traumatic false belief from early childhood that I was "unlovable." It seemed validated when a Red Cross volunteer had said to me: "God must not be on your side" when I told her my address. "My friends live on that street and their home didn't burn." Rattled and spiraling down emotionally, I began to believe that somehow, she was right; despite how unrealistic and irrational that thought was.

Needing to peel away and correct more underlying layers of these unconscious false beliefs about myself, I returned to therapy. Soon thereafter, a colleague and friend invited me to join her at a workshop using a new modality called "equine therapy."

We drove to Descanso to meet our leader and the other participants. After choosing a horse for the day, my years of equine experience betrayed me as mine would not lead properly. "He's showing you how you don't believe in yourself and have poor boundaries," the facilitator added.

Humbled, I was discovering the value of allowing a sentient animal to reflect my process. Next, I was to walk through the area with all the horses and enter the round pen where my chosen steed was waiting for my next "lesson." As I slowly walked, the facilitator asked me to silently repeat my question, "Am I lovable?"

"I feel like something is behind me."

"Look around," she offered. Every single horse in that pen was following me closely. They stopped when I paused to turn around but did not break their formation behind me. Tears wet my cheeks as I took this in and then was encouraged to enter the round pen where my mentor was waiting.

Standing ten feet away with his rear end toward me, I silently repeated my question. Seconds later, he turned and slowly approached. Leaning toward my head, he bent his down and softly nuzzled my cheek with his horse lips.

"He just kissed me." Again, tears slid down my cheeks as I stroked his head and thanked him. His message delivered, he looked me in the eyes, backed away and turned around. Resuming his position, he again stood with his head pointing away from me.

"He just confirmed that I'm loveable! From a horse no less."

I left the round pen to join the others and share with them the question I had asked my horse. I was not the only one moved to tears with the joy of my experience; they were equally touched with this wonderful affirmation given me by my equine mentor.

Flashpoints of Awareness

That day, I discovered once again our inner connectedness with all living beings. Indeed, I had entered Einstein's "unified field;" reawakened to the love that is our ground of being.

Leaving San Pasqual

I grew up in San Pasqual Valley on my family's dairy farm. We enjoyed two ranches in the valley nestled amidst the surrounding hills, flowing rivers, and lush vegetation. Olive trees lined the road connecting family members and the other dairies but was mostly only traveled by tractors, horses, and locals. We knew the comings and goings of folks by the sound of their vehicles as they putzed along the road at a slow ten miles per hour. The highway across the valley was reserved for traffic moving from the mountains to the east through the valley and into the small town of Escondido.

The prodigy of two pioneer families, I am the fifth generation to live there. In 1875, my paternal great-great grandfather traveled out West from the New England area and settled in the valley.

They lived peacefully among the San Pasqual Indians who are part of the Kumeyaay. His only daughter, Elizabeth Judson Roberts became an advocate for them and authored a book dictated by members of their tribe to preserve their history.

In the endless cycle of dominant forces oppressing those with a seemingly lesser voice, the sheriff from the city of San Diego burned down their village. Forced from their ancestral homes, they followed the pathway up the Guejito River (Rockwood Canyon) and found refuge near Lake Wohlford. That is how the "San Pasqual Indians" ended up near Valley Center.

In the late 1950s, thirteen of my family members were part of a total of seventeen plaintiffs who sued the city of San Diego for violating their water rights with the construction of the Sutherland Dam that had dropped their water tables. The judgment against the City awarded the farmers a million dollars in damages. However, instead of paying, the City forced them to sell their land through eminent domain. The farmers received a pittance of what their land was worth.

Leaving San Pasqual

    Although my paternal grandfather was among those who lost claim to the land they had farmed for over eighty-four years, Assemblyman Phillip D. Swing, a friend of his, brokered an extraordinary agreement with the City allowing my grandparents to continue living in their home for fifty years or the duration of their lifetimes. Our grandmother lived to be well over 105 years old, allowing us to enjoy our heritage until her demise. Unfortunately, our grandfather passed away from a fatal heart attack shortly after the papers were signed.

    I was the last of our family to enjoy the blessings of our pristine valley. In 2007, the remnants of my family's presence went up in smoke with the Witch Creek Fire. Both the original home built in 1880 and my grandparents' residence constructed in 1890 by my grandfather's father were consumed along with the ranch buildings. My home I had lived in for a year was also gutted; the adobe walls standing as stark reminders of what was. As narrated in my book, *Sanity Lost and Found: A True Story of Brainwashing and Recovery*, I recklessly entered the flames of that inferno, placing myself in a life-threatening situation as I tried in vain to save my home. After helplessly watching everything burn, it took me years to finally surrender the notion of rebuilding and replanting my grove. Nothing was as it had been—it was time to move on.

    Gone were the cottonwoods and oaks lining the floor of the valley along with the trees and other lush foliage from a former time. Raw and exposed, the valley became a thoroughfare for the increasing traffic from the east, looking for a shortcut to the interstate. Racing around the curvy roads became a contest for fast cars and heavy feet pressed hard on the accelerator. Ignoring the young children occupying the surviving houses perched on the road's shoulder, these drivers had made the road a dangerous speedway.

My learning process continued when the listing of my property was confounded with the ancient Homestead Act deed of trust and the ensuing reenactment of water rights disputes with the city of San Diego. Discovering that all the water rights lawyers in the county had business ties with the city of San Diego, I hired someone from a Pasadena firm.

Shortly thereafter, he called me. "It is clearly stated in the legal documents that your ancestors trusted they had guaranteed water rights for your property into perpetuity. However, the City is using the contaminated well to void that legal document."

"How can this be? This isn't right! For over thirty years, the City has leased the bottom land to a commercial citrus grower. The chemical fertilizers they used contaminated the underground aquifer along with my well. The City is responsible for allowing my well to be contaminated."

"Yes, but because that well no longer has potable water, the City is maintaining the legal agreement is now void and no longer valid. With the sale of your land, you will lose your right to pump water up your hill from the source below."

Generational rage surged through me. Despite my previous efforts to forgive the past, ugly feelings I had harbored and thought forgiven and released, stirred within me once again. I was revisiting our family's shared malcontent with the land seizure and years of having to remind the City of their responsibility as landlords to properly maintain our grandmother's and the other historical homes they had appropriated.

"Why can't we just sue them?" I asked, exasperated with this news.

"Because they will take your land through eminent domain like they did with your ancestors," my lawyer responded.

"How can I be fighting this same battle fifty-five years later? Can't we sue them for allowing my well to become contaminated?"

"That would take years of litigation and you are not likely to win. There is only one case that has been settled despite all the numerous complaints filed against municipalities and agribusinesses contaminating groundwater supplies." (As of 2016)

"This is so difficult to hear. Can't we do anything?"

"What water source does your property have now?"

"When a child developed a problem with his kidneys, they tested the water and discovered the contamination. The original homestead, my grandmother's home, the dairy and its ranch houses, the Academy, and mine—were all tapped into a different well farther upstream and free of contamination. Because the Academy was leasing the original homestead along with our old dairy and ranch houses at the time, we were all included in the new system since they were a public institution and legally required to supply potable water. My well was then officially designated for agricultural use only."

"Well, that's quite a story. Let me see what we can negotiate with the City. Your ancestors signed away their riparian rights in the legal document, in exchange for the ongoing rights to your contaminated well on their former property, now owned by the City. There might be something we can do."

Over the next two years, as my lawyer dialogued with the City through various proposals and rebuttals, I prayed diligently for assistance from Spirit in resolving this matter, and in releasing my negative thoughts and emotions about it all. Most of all my anger, as I knew that would not help me.

"Good news," the email stated. "You are now free to drill a well on your property. Call me so we can discuss this."

I could not have expressed my gratitude enough to my lawyer and to Spirit with this wonderful miracle. After contacting a well driller for my next step, we walked the length of my lot together.

Pointing to the east end, I explained, "I'd like you to drill for water here."

"Why would you want to drill there? That's on a bank and the other end looks like it would be more promising in finding water."

"Well, I did some water witching on the entire property and discovered there is a source of water here. I also consulted some geological maps and there should be an underground stream about here."

"Hmm. It's going to be difficult to get my rig over there, but I'll try."

"I appreciate that. I really need a well. If I sell my land, my water rights do not transfer to the new owner because I will lose the right to pump water through those pipes. And I can't sell the land without water."

"I don't understand, can't you just replace the burned parts and use that line?" He pointed to the pipeline running up from the former ranch to my water tank.

'I wish it were that easy. The firestorm exposed and then burned the pipe but it's much more complicated than that." And I proceeded to explain the entire debacle and the past two years' dispute with the city of San Diego.

"Wow, that is challenging. How deep do you want me to drill to find water?"

"Please start drilling and let me know your progress, okay?"

"Sure. I might have to go really deep."

"Whatever it takes at this point. Thank you."

We scheduled the work to start on the thirtieth of March. Several days later I received a call.

"I found water at 280 feet, flowing at about one gallon per minute." (GPM)

"That's pretty miserable, isn't it?"

"Yes, ma'am."

"Okay, please keep drilling."

He called the next day. "Tarra, I'm down to 427 feet and only getting two gallons per minute."

"Please keep drilling."

"Yes, ma'am."

"Oh man, do I have any guilt left in my mind about selling this land? What about my anger with the City, haven't I let it all go? What's making this so difficult? There's supposed to be water there. I asked Spirit and the ancestors to assist me, and I've been mindful of my negative thoughts and feelings—practicing forgiveness. Please, Spirit, please help me in forgiving this process."

Several days later, I received a call from the well driller that was much different.

"Tarra, I'm at 645 feet and getting 32 gallons per minute. That now makes a total of 35 gallons per minute from that well!!!"

"WooHoo!! That's great! Thank you!" Silently, I thanked Spirit.

"Do you know the best part?"

"No, what's that?"

"I had the water tested and it's 100 percent pure. It's not contaminated like the aquifer!"

"Oh, my goodness! That's so cool. Thank you! Thank you, thank you!"

A few years later as I was leaving my bank, a former neighbor pulled up beside me and rolled down her window. I leaned in closer, "How do you like your new neighbors that bought my place?"

"They're great. We like them. Did you know that he got permission to pump water up the hill? He's using your old pipeline."

"No. You're kidding."

"Nope, it's true. Apparently, the City gave him permission to reconnect into our water system."

"Ha, ha, ha! That is hilarious! Oh, that's too funny and how totally ironic!! Oh well. I'm glad for them."

Walking back to my car, I remembered the power of forgiveness; what happens when we let go of our emotions and attachments to an outcome. *"I sold the land, got through some very ugly emotions, and got my miracle. I am so grateful for all that. Thank you, Spirit!"*

Ma'am

My friend greeted me as I opened the door. "Tarra, you're wearing a skirt. I don't think I've ever seen you wear a skirt! Why are you so dressed up for our meeting?"

"Well, I was told that tonight they're honoring our group for having completed the four-year post graduate somatic psychology program. I wanted to look my best."

"Cool. Do you still need to pick up the dessert you're taking?"

"Yes, it will only take a minute and it's on the way to San Diego. I'm ready, want to leave?"

As I pulled into the store, I asked, "Do you want to come in with me?"

"No, I'll just stay here in the car."

Walking inside, I strutted across the aisles and over to the bakery section. *"Look at me, I'm styling"* I thought to myself as I waited at the counter. Seconds later, a woman walked up behind me and leaned over, whispering in her southern accent.

"Ma'am. Excuse me, ma'am. Your skirt is tucked up into your pantyhose."

"Oh God. Thank you for telling me" I muttered as I rushed to sit down in a nearby chair. I frantically tugged at my skirt to loosen it from the confines of my pantyhose while an elderly gentleman looked on, quite puzzled with what I was doing.

Still parked in my chair after making some final adjustments, my guardian angel walked past me, nodding as she did. "Thank you!" I whispered.

After picking out the dessert, I furtively paid and tried slinking past the personnel who had previously witnessed my unintended show.

"You won't believe what happened to me!" I blurted out as I got into the car.

"What?"

As I explained my embarrassment, uproarious laughter took over us both, especially when I shared how sassy I had felt as I walked across the store to the dessert counter.

"I can't believe it. I don't know if I will ever be able to go into that store again!"

"Oh, of course you will, Tarra."

"Well, maybe next year." And we burst into laughter again. "What is the saying? 'Pride cometh before a fall.' Well, that was definitely a face plant!"

More laughter ensued as we enjoyed the drive to our meeting.

Pause for Reflection

In our full lives, it seems we seldom take the opportunity to pause and notice our surroundings, much less spend time in reflection. While enjoying my coffee this morning, I spied an unusual movement of the tree branches near my fence. Moving outside to investigate, a mother possum, with her babies clinging tightly, was hovering among the branches wispily offering her camouflage.

I retreated to watch from behind a window as she inched along the branch and dropped down to hide behind my wood pile. The gardeners next door had apparently flushed her out and she was seeking refuge.

I have a bit of "undeveloped" land near me, thus attracting such wandering creatures as mother possum. I feel blessed as I grew up in the luxury of natural surroundings, and have found a place to live, somewhat free of the proximity of humans living next door.

While looking for mother possum, who is still out of sight, I wonder. *"How strange, this word 'undeveloped,' I think it means free of humans and their impact. As I hide behind my window, within the protection of my home, I'm insulated from nature. But how often in our protection from it, do we compete with those who share our planet? Do we humans need to conquer and tame the land around us? Is it natural for us, or perhaps something we can question and change?"*

We have tamed animals as pets and control nature through our landscaping, but what funny creatures we are to insist on demonstrating our ability to dominate others. In fact, there are no "others," rather we are all living, breathing creatures sharing this ship hurling through the ocean of space.

When we have met the basics for survival, perhaps that's when the responsibility for exercising love, acceptance, and generosity is the next step in OUR development, rather than

Pause for Reflection

staying in the fight, flight, freeze mode of controlling, getting, and reacting.

Pausing in this present moment, mother possum's gift offers gratitude rising within me. As I appreciate this mindful opportunity, I feel love for her, a way to connect with my Self—our true nature—not the reactive emotional behaviors our survival-oriented brains generate.

Rather than working so hard to destroy nature, perhaps we could benefit more from taming our mindless tendencies to judge rather than accept. We never know the miracles we could enjoy until we do.

The Camino

In March of 2014, I sat with about fifty others in a La Jolla conference room, listening to David Whyte present various poems from around the world as he challenged us to look within to discover ourselves. I marveled at his ability to recite poem after poem, first in their original language and then in English, repeating certain lines for emphasis. His recitations were punctuated with questions.

Flashpoints of Awareness

"What kind of an invitation am I to the world? What is my relationship to the Great Silence? The edge, as the sensor of where I end and begin."

Enraptured, I listened to the musings of famous poets who contemplated life's mysteries and beyond, and feverishly recorded bits of his presentation along with my own responses.

"Just crack your heart—the conversation will do the rest . . . The pilgrimage, the necessity to ask for help, walking into the unknown, ask for invisible help—the help you do not, as yet know you need . . . You have to shape an identity that is ripe and ready to survive . . . What temporary name might you want to take on or what new name might you want to use?"

"Hmm. I've needed to ask for help plenty of times and, indeed, I've already taken on several new names in my life as I tried reinventing myself."

"What is the nature of your reluctance?"

"I don't have enough time to write all that out."

"You have to greet new parts and old ones that are leaving, breaking your heart. Paulo Coelho wrote of the Pilgrimage . . . Go into retreat while you walk El Camino . . . Start with the first step you don't want to take."

I wrote the following: *"The step I don't want to take—finish my book with personal references to my insanity, what I went through and how I came out of it. And, how I dropped back into it when I was faced with losing my home to the fire—that I plunged into the fire and then suffered with all the loss until I could come back to myself."*

David continued, "Start with the ground you know . . . Don't let them smother your own voice. Don't follow someone else's voice, listen to your own."

"Oh, that so applies to me! The end of this step will be to do only what is loving for me; what I have learned, listening to a different part of me like my heart and intuition, not my ego mind."

As he narrated the onslaught of provocative poems and excerpts, he also shared a poem he wrote for his niece. A recent university graduate, she was going to walk the Camino, a pilgrimage trail in Spain.

A memory stirred within me as I listened. *"I have always wanted to walk the Camino. What would it be like to be a simple 'peregrina' without the alphabet soup after my name? No one would know that I'm a therapist, or anything about me. To walk into the unknown, like he said. Hmm, I wonder what that would be like?"* So moved by the entire experience, I raised my hand to share and then heard myself publicly commit to walking the "Camino de Santiago."

I left November sixth of that same year for my "spiritual journey." Landing in Paris, our bus drove through rush hour traffic to the airport in Orly. Lourdes was my next destination.

The rainy, cold weather failed to dampen my spirits as I entered the Sanctuary of Our Lady of Lourdes. Despite the inclement weather, the church was full. I quietly stood in the back as there was a mass in progress. *"This is a beautiful cathedral. I must have seen hundreds of canes and crutches on my way here, discarded relics from the faithful. I guess they were rewarded for their belief in the possibility of miracles from visiting this place. I hope I experience some on my Camino."*

The train schedule had not been updated since the tourist season, so my planned departure was delayed for most of the day. I wandered around the town of Lourdes and found a restaurant where I enjoyed a formal lunch of French cuisine. Disappointed that almost everything was closed, I mused, *"Note to self, don't come here again on a Sunday."*

We boarded the last train in the very late afternoon. Jet-lagged, I dozed off and on until arriving at Bonneville, my next stop. Standing in front of a closed bathroom, I wondered what I would do with my growing need. Someone walked up next to me, apparently also in disbelief with the locked doors.

"El Camino?" I nodded. "English, yes," she added. However, we understood each other better in Spanish. Spying a restaurant closing for the night, I motioned for her to follow. The kind owner allowed us to use his restroom, refused payment, and was profusely thanked.

Returning the favor, Catalina helped me validate my tickets for our next train which would take us to the bus station for Saint Jean-Pied-de-Port. Aboard the bus, we wove back and forth up the mountains until arriving around 11:00 p.m. The driver stopped in the center of town and was greeted by a deranged man yelling about something. He approached the driver, kissed both his cheeks, and walked way. Catalina and I looked at each other in amazement and then she showed the driver her map. "Can you take us to this rooming house?"

"I cannot see well enough to read that. Get in and I will take you there."

Rather puzzled, nonetheless we dutifully boarded and were dropped off at the edge of town. The bus driver was incorrigible despite our requests to return us to the original bus stop. Gratefully, Catalina had GPS to guide us through the rain as we walked back to the central and her hostel. "You are welcome to stay here but there is no guarantee of a bed. You can ring the manager and see."

I thanked her for her kindness and explained that I had paid for a room somewhere else. We parted ways and I retraced our steps and found the residencia. There was a note on the door stating I had to get my key from a certain restaurant in town.

It had stopped raining when I found the only open place and inquired where the restaurant could be found. The bartender kindly directed me, warning me to avoid the deranged man walking the streets. "Yes, I have seen him," I explained and found the restaurant. I walked in to find the owners counting out their money.

"We are so glad to see you! We are closing and about to leave. We called you several times, but no one answered." Without explaining that I didn't have international service so could not get their calls, I apologized for their troubles and gratefully took my keys.

Leaving the next morning, I passed through the stone archway at the end of their town as a local woman walked through in the opposite direction. "Would you like me to take your picture?" She asked.

"Yes, thank you."

She was French but also spoke Spanish. Pleasantries were exchanged after she took my picture, and she continued walking on her way. Filled with resolve, I headed to the trail through the Pyrenees mountains. *"And off I go."*

No more than twenty steps later, a man walked outside his house on the hill above me. "Hello, you do not want to go that way. There is snow on the trail and people have died on it for the extreme weather. Go that way instead. It's longer but much safer!" he said, pointing to a trail on the right. Another opportunity to thank someone for his generosity.

Walking along the path, I occasionally paused to admire the surrounding greenery and drink in the sounds of the river. Lessening more and more was the chatter within my mind. The path continued onto a paved road and besides two Shetland ponies grazing on the shoulder, I was alone with this reawakened peaceful feeling.

When I overtook a tall Canadian man, my solitude was broken as he accompanied me, sharing his stories. "I was in the hospital for ten months with a brain disorder. They didn't know if I would survive. And now I'm walking the Camino. I'm looking for a miracle."

"Seems to me that may have been your miracle. What an incredible story."

I soon tired of his nonstop talking and feigned needing to attend to a blister on my foot, encouraging him to walk on ahead. After waiting a while, I started again and stopped at a local restaurant to give him more time to get far ahead of me. Fascinated, I listened as the patrons easily switched from French to Spanish in their conversations. "What country are we in please?" I asked in Spanish.

"This is Spain. We are on the border between Spain and France."

I marveled at the simplicity between these two countries with their boundaries. *How delightful. So, unlike the struggles my country has with its borders.*

The Pyrenees mountains loomed ahead as the Camino route led me off the paved road. Slipping on the wet ground as the path grew steeper and more difficult, I was humbled to see a couple roaming about, effortlessly gathering mushrooms. Their small cabin sat off the trail, nestled among the trees.

Eventually dropping down on the other side, I wandered into the cluster of buildings and noticed a hotel boasting a billboard in front, "Martin Sheen stayed here." After walking inside, I decided it was not for me and left. Outside, I happened to catch a glimpse of the Canadian walking into the hostel and was glad he made it over the mountains. The delightful scent of food drew me to a small chateau-like building, next to the hostel.

"We have a small room upstairs you can rent for the night" I was told. "And we can wash and press your clothes for you and have them ready for you this evening," the man at the desk offered, spying my mud-stained pants. "You are welcome to join us for dinner," he added.

My hosts were a husband and wife who worked tirelessly that night welcoming and serving delicious meals to the onslaught of travelers stopping there.

Fortified with great food and styling clean clothes, I continued through the miles and nights until joining a small group I met at one of the hostels. A couple from Ireland and a woman from Italy became my companions as we trekked, eventually reaching Pamplona where the bulls are run. We opted for hotel rooms and to meet later at a local restaurant. After getting lost and wandering around, wishing again I had cell service, I ran into Lucia from our group who then escorted me to the restaurant. We were joined that night by Lucia's friend, another woman from Italy who introduced herself to our group. "Hello, my name is Silvia Bussi."

The next morning, Silvia, the Irish couple, and I climbed the hill leading out of Pamplona. Lucia had already left much earlier. Speaking four languages and English very fluently, Silvia and I discovered many similarities in our upbringing and shared interests, despite the differences in age and country.

The next albergue (hostel) would be our last night with the Irish couple as they were returning home. Lucia continued to leave very early, powering on like an energizer bunny so Silvia and I walked together. Soon, despite my lovely connection with her, I was entertaining an ego desire to traverse as many miles as my short time allowed, wanting bragging rights for the miles. She did not walk as fast as I would have liked so I decided to leave her and walk on ahead.

"I have truly enjoyed our time together, but I'd like to walk as many miles as possible since I don't have much time. I've decided to walk on ahead and hope to see you at the next albergue. You have Lucia, so you will not be completely alone. Buen Camino, it's been so fun to share with you."

And with that, I charged up the hill before me. About three-fourths of the way to the top I distinctly heard a voice inside me say, "Tarra, what are you doing? You're leaving a completely trusted friend to brag about how many miles you traveled?"

"*Oh, you're right!*" I answered. "*I guess I'm being an ass.*" And with that, I turned around and walked back down the hill, stopping in front of Silvia.

"I'm sorry. I realized that I was not being kind and would like to continue walking with you, no matter how long it takes. Would you forgive me for leaving you?"

"Yes, of course. Let's make it a photo tour and take whatever time it takes."

"That sounds great, thank you."

We ambled along, taking pictures of the multicolored grape leaves in the Rioja, with its beautiful surrounding countryside. Silvia started gathering various plants as we continued walking,

"I am delighted to find all these herbs that are so good for cooking."

"I'm impressed that you know the names of so many. I only recognize this one—sage."

When we arrived at the albergue, there was quite a crowd that were staying for the night. Lucia was among them.

"If you would not mind getting these groceries, I will prepare a meal for all of us," Silvia offered as she handed me a shopping list. Lucia helped me find the items and another pilgrim purchased several bottles of fine European wine. He was from Bulgaria, preparing to hike the Kilimanjaro Mountain.

When Silvia brought forth our feast, a toast was made, and we filled our plates. Tears rolled down my cheeks as I savored my first bite.

"Tarra, you're crying" Silvia noted. "Are you alright?"

"Oh yes. This is so heavenly, thank you."

As I savored another bite, I realized the depth of gratitude I was feeling. *"This is such delicious food and I'm so glad I chose to stay with Silvia rather than pursue my silly desire to rack up more miles."*

My dear friend Silvia and I have since traveled together several times, each journey better than the last.

Eddie

Leaving for the night, I loaded my purse and briefcase onto my shoulder and unlocked the front door. Stepping across the threshold, I turned around to lock the door behind me and jumped with the sight of someone sitting on the patio bench to my left.

"Oh, you startled me!"

"Do you want me to leave?"

"No, no, that's okay. I just didn't expect anyone to be here."

Flashpoints of Awareness

I studied this frightened young man dressed in army fatigues. Probably in his late twenties, he was cradling a laptop; a cell phone was plugged in next to him on the bench. I continued the conversation.

"Are you a veteran?"

"Yes, ma'am."

"Oh, I've never seen you before. Where do you normally stay?"

"I sleep around on friends' couches."

"What about your benefits from the VA? I hope they're helping you."

"No, ma'am, it's a big mess there and I'm still waiting."

"Oh, my, that's too bad. I'm sorry it's taking them so long. My name is Tarra. You're welcome to sleep here just so long as you clean up after yourself and don't stay here when we're open for business."

"Yes, ma'am, thank you, ma'am. My name is Eddie, ma'am."

"Okay, nice to meet you, Eddie. And you don't have to call me ma'am, just Tarra."

"Yes, ma'am."

"Stay safe and have a good night, Eddie."

"Thank you, ma'am.

About a month later, one of the neighbors from the apartment building next door called the office to say that she had been bringing Eddie food and hoped that was okay. "I feel safer when he's sleeping in the patio."

Eddie

"That's very kind of you. He's a veteran and I told him he could sleep in the patio. He doesn't make any noise, does he?"

"Oh, no. He's very quiet. The only way I know he's there, is I can see his boots from my window."

As the months passed, we conversed whenever he was there as I left the office for the night.

"Eddie, haven't you received your benefits yet?

"No, ma'am."

"It's getting colder during the night. I hope that you get some help soon. Did you know that Interfaith Community Services has a program for homeless veterans? They're down on Washington Street. Maybe you could go see them and get some help. They have all kinds of resources. They'll even give you a sack lunch and help you find shelter. Seems like it would certainly be better than braving this cold."

"Yes, ma'am. Okay, ma'am."

"Please take care of yourself and get some help."

"Yes, ma'am."

Weeks later, Eddie was sitting on the bench, bundled against the cold. "Eddie, this is no way to live. Has the VA helped you out yet?

"No, ma'am."

"Oh, good grief. Do you have family somewhere?"

'Yes, ma'am. They're back East."

"Don't you think they might be worried about you? Is there some way that you can reach out to them for some help?"

"Well, I guess so, ma'am."

"I encourage you to reach out to them. Please, Eddie. It's going to keep getting colder each night and you shouldn't have to live like this. Is there anything I can do to help?"

"No, ma'am. I'll be okay."

"Please, please take care of yourself."

"Yes, ma'am."

A year had passed without seeing Eddie when someone using the office reported seeing him leave in the morning. "I was afraid to unlock the door when I saw him sleeping on the bench. He woke up and ran out of the patio. He was so tall and homeless looking."

"Yes, he's a veteran and a good person. He's harmless and I told him he could spend the night in the patio so long as he left before we opened."

"Well, he scared one of my clients when he abruptly stood up and ran away."

The next morning, I caught Eddie's eye as he bolted away after awakening from the bench. He was no longer the same easygoing young man I had known. With hair and clothes in disarray, he sprinted from the patio like a wild animal.

After hearing the complaints and fears from the other clinicians using the building, I realized that things needed to change. Sadly, I removed the bench from the alcove and replaced it with a large horse trough filled with potted plants. There was still another bench in the patio, but it was visible from the street and not conducive to overnight sleeping.

I often think about Eddie and wonder what ever happened to him. I pray his benefits finally came through and that he was given assistance to get back on his feet and work through whatever trauma the war had subjected him to.

Why is it that we expect those who cannot make the journey toward help, to do so on their own? Thousands of feet had crossed the threshold of our offices, seeking support and assistance with their life situations. But they had the awareness and capability to reach out and find what they needed. I do not know what trauma and damage to his psyche Eddie had sustained in the war and his life. I pray for him and do not judge his inability to seek help instead of slowly deteriorating, losing more of his humanity with each day spent on the street.

I also pray for forgiveness for whatever unconscious guilt in my mind may have contributed to his plight and the suffering of other homeless and mentally unwell individuals. I do believe the answer is not in judging, self or other, but in recognizing that compassion and forgiveness are the most important healing factors for all those wary and wandering souls who've fallen through the cracks in our societal fabric.

Another Transition

Transitions can be from conscious choice or like when a rock hits the windshield, and your vision is impaired as the crack grows. Rocks have hit the windshield of my awareness numerous times. The shock and emotional turmoil I experienced each time was a bout of amnesia—forgetting that I have survived countless times despite my fears.

Twenty-nine years ago, I began anew as a psychotherapist. This was a significant leap for me, previously having been tremendously compromised. While in a cult to "help save the world" I was a transient homeless person. Having missed more than a decade of my family history, I struggled to release my guilt and sadness for having missed so much. Now, I was learning to watch with appreciation and witness family members grow, marry, and move away.

More lessons of letting go and accepting "what is" occurred when my only sibling, my champion and dear brother, dropped dead at forty-seven of a heart related issue. He left behind three children, a loving wife, and a gaping hole in my heart. That was by far my most difficult transition to accept. He was joining others in my large extended family who had preceded him in death. Reluctantly, I was learning that change is a daily fare.

Several years later, my father's avocado grove and our childhood home became my inheritance. Splitting myself between the trees and my private practice, I wore two hats then. When the Witch Creek Fire consumed my home, the grove, and our grandmother's house along with the surrounding ranch buildings, I was devastated. However, as the pain of my loss abated, I began to see that the remodeling I had done was another attempt to rewrite our familial history. I had buried myself again in this "correction" when in fact, maintaining both had been exhaustive and self-destructive.

Now, without the validation of these physical symbols with all the memories they represented, I had the opportunity to

Another Transition

let go and join the present moment. If I could embrace this, there would be no need for "corrections" to be made, for everything that happened had brought me to this present moment. Regardless of my previous efforts, I could now choose to transform my perception of it all. In other words, I had the potential to be free and have peace of mind.

Until these symbols of my worth were destroyed, I had failed to recognize that it was my mind's thinking that needed to change. Toward that end, I welcomed the support of therapy, loving friends, family, and my higher power.

Moving from the country to suburbia, I let go of farming, settled into my home, and continued my practice. I had no idea that such a transition could start so traumatically and end up being so sweet. Surrendering to it all had revealed its benefits to me.

The end of 2021 was yet another challenge as I stepped across a new threshold toward retirement. Despite feeling guided in this, I struggled to let go and wrestled with my core unwillingness. My profession had been so incredibly nurturing, and I was very clear that I was not doing the work, rather I had offered myself to Spirit as an instrument for healing. I felt truly humbled and so honored with the trust given me by the people with whom I had worked. I could not see how in this next chapter that I would be of service and experience the love and gratitude I had felt for others.

Tears and more tears followed as I said goodbye to cherished clients, dear colleagues, and twenty years in my cottage office. Dismantling and clearing the space for its next life, I was reluctantly leaving its comforting familiarity and the grounding effect of my routines.

As I slogged through my process, I fought off fears whether I had done a "good enough job." Essentially, I was revisiting a childhood false belief of "not being good enough." I believe this came from my perception and misinterpretation of the emotional deprivation during our developmental years, assuming the love I craved was not forthcoming for my lack of worthiness. Children usually blame themselves for the anomalies in their environment. Truly, this became another opportunity to grow and forgive what had seemed to occur in my youth. Our parents were doing the best they could, and no one would benefit from blaming or shaming them.

As this process continued, more false perceptions were squeezed to the surface to be healed. I started doubting my previous retirement calculations, *"Will I be able to support myself financially moving forward?"* looped through my brain. *"Am I going to be all right facing this unknown?"* was another fear hijacking me.

Alone in my nightmare, my resistance had exhausted me by the end of my last week of working and served to fuel more self-absorbed pity and fears. Knowing I could not manage my issues by myself, I prayed for assistance as I spiraled down the rabbit hole. *"Holy Spirit, please help me surrender to this process and please help me forgive all these fears and guilt I'm entertaining."*

"Trust me" I heard above my sobs.

From that point forward, I surrendered to this next step, realizing that my intention to discipline the nonsense in my mind was yet another reason for retirement. *"I have been the sacrificial lamb, my suffering self-imposed. But what will become of all this love I have shared with others? Is it possible to love myself with some of that same force, and rest with a calmed mind, digesting the stillness of each moment I no longer need to fill?"*

Gently, I was being lured from the cave of my blinded perceptions, as the light drew me near its source—Love. *"You have gifted me a clear mind again. I know I am going to be all right and trust I did the best I could. Aah, Spirit, thank you once again! My mind is at peace and filled with love. I am learning more and more to surrender to you. How silly I can be at times."*

Exercises for Self-Regulation and Forgiveness

You may ask why forgiveness is so important, and what is it, exactly. First of all, forgiveness is not about someone doing something wrong to you and, in your benevolence, you forgive them. That is a subtle way of blaming someone with guilt for victimizing you. In reality, projecting that guilt onto them ensures that the guilt in some negative form will return to you. (What goes around, comes around). Or, from the *Course in Miracles*: "Ideas leave not their source."

Attempting to analyze and figure out why you are so upset about a situation, why it happened, who is to blame and so on, is another way of denying our present moment experience. If you recognize that within this holographic experience, whatever comes to us is an unlearned lesson, then we become the ones responsible for what is before us.

Shakespeare knew this when he cautioned us against obsessing (analyzing) our problems through the words of King Lear: "that way madness lies."

If we choose to use our right-minds (our Spirit, or Higher Power) when facing this challenge, we have the possibility of neutralizing it by not reacting, not attacking another, and not ensuring its return. The Holy Spirit, or Spirit, is that spark of divinity that is the essence of our being which is God's perfect love. Asking for assistance from the Holy Spirit is choosing our right-minds, which will lead us through the emotional upset, (acceptance) to forgiveness (neutralizing it). Thus, we have chosen to free ourselves from the potential of more bondage within this illusion represented by the subsequent consequences that ego-minded choices bring.

Emotions are hormonally driven reactions to certain events generated by our ego-mind and then translated through the brain/body. These defenses (emotions), based on our negative perceptions of events, hijack our inner peace. At every given moment, we have the power to choose and decide which mind we utilize in our responses. If we view these negative experiences as learning opportunities rather than assuming victimization or judgment, we open the door to higher awareness. To facilitate the higher learning afforded by these opportunities, the Holy Spirit is at our beck and call. All we need to do is ask.

Again, to ensure the repetition of these lessons, we can also choose to react emotionally with our ego defenses and judgments. The following are some simple steps for employing an accelerated process for one's learning curriculum. Even when we have reacted with our ego-minds, we are forgiven of our mistakes when we ask for assistance in learning from it, correcting, and being forgiven for it.

We are human beings and will often times react emotionally or automatically judge. The importance lies in recognizing our lapse into ego-minded thinking and behaving and asking for assistance in returning to our right-minds. These are the mistakes through which we progress and reclaim our true selves.

1. **For any emotional state, first move away from the stimulating factor. Take a time out and find safety. Be practical, take care of yourself:**
   - Ask Spirit for assistance as soon as you recognize an emotion has replaced your peace of mind.
   - Take slow, deep breaths and, if possible, place your feet flat on the ground.
   - Put a hand over your heart and the other one on your lower belly as you breathe slowly and mindfully.
   - Notice what you are feeling and thinking.
   - Ask the Holy Spirit to assist you in accepting and releasing the emotion you are feeling and any related negative judgments.

- If you know someone who is nonjudgmental and accepting, seek support from them as you relate your recognition of your experience.

- Remember that emotions are not who we are, they are temporary states of feelings that serve to distract us away from our right-minds, serving to cause further dysregulation and a lack of inner peace.

2. **Anger:**
   - Move away from the offending person or situation. Use this energy to find safety.
   - Make sure to release your breath and ask for help from the Holy Spirit.
   - We usually are not angry for the reasons we think, it is more often from a past injury needing correction.
   - Remember to blame someone or something for your anger is to give it or them your power and become a victim.
   - You have a right to express that you are feeling anger about thus and so but need to be willing to let it go.
   - Take responsibility for your part in this.

- Forgive the other or ask for assistance in forgiving if you find yourself struggling to find your peace of mind in the situation.
- If you act out your anger on someone or something, in essence, you are attacking yourself since we are all one.
- Judgments are another form of attack.
- Attack causes guilt which then causes some form of circular behavior in the form of self-punishment, negative events returning, and so on. (i.e., karma)
- Often times, we react automatically. If you have done so, remember it is merely a mistake and it can be neutralized by asking for assistance from the Holy Spirit to forgive yourself.

3. **For Fears/Sadness/Depression:**
    - Remember we are never really alone.
    - Ask for assistance from Spirit.
    - Since we have free choice and free will, the Holy Spirit will not impose Itself on us but comes only when invited.

4. Anxiety:

- Anxiety is a form of fear when not trusting the reality that you are safe in the present moment.

- Anxiety may hijack you from a previously suppressed fearful and traumatic event.

- Anxiety may also happen when you obsess (mindlessly think) about something from the past or the future, rather than being present in the here and now.

- Breathe deeply and ask for assistance from Spirit to get back into your right mind (the here and now).

- Notice any feelings and judgments accompanying this experience and ask for assistance in releasing them.

- Continue to breathe in a normal, rhythmical fashion. (In for four counts, pause for four, out for four, and pause for four. Repeat the process again until you feel balanced and at peace. It is not important to count to four, feel free to count to any number without causing stress). You can also imagine drawing a square with your breathing, giving your brain something else to think rather than the stimulating issue.

Exercises for Self-Regulation and Forgiveness

- Obsessive thinking will cause anxiety (fear) whether it is about your future or the past.
- Think of FEAR as False Evidence Appearing as Real. It is part of the illusion we live in.
- Fear is the opposite of love (trust).

5. Whatever is in front of you in the present moment is an unlearned lesson:

- It has come to you to be corrected (learned), and then released through forgiveness so that it does not return and create more disturbance in your life.
- Stored within the unconscious part of our mind are all the mindless thoughts and behaviors we have experienced.
- Because we were not "mindful" (right-minded) about learning that lesson, it has returned.
- If we projected it, guilt would be the result. That guilt ensures repetition which means it needs recognition and forgiveness (neutralization).
- If we denied it (stuffed it into our unconscious mind), it will also return much like a sliver that festers in our skin until it is removed.
- Asking for assistance from the Holy Spirit is a

fail-safe way of working through and learning our lessons.

- Please remember it will always be about forgiveness, no matter what.
- Forgiveness returns us to our right-mind, that state of love and acceptance that brings peace of mind and a sense of well-being.

Acknowledgments

FOR THE PRODUCTION of this book, it has been my pleasure to receive the assistance and support of my illustrator, Joel Paola, and the graphic design expertise of Gwyn Flowers of GKS Creative who designed the book covers and interior layout for me. Self-publishing a book is indeed a community project, and I am also very grateful to Tony Bonds of Golden Ratio Book Design for his kind assistance. My dear friends Donna Johnson, Mary Brutger, and Susan Schoeppner generously gave of their time in helping with creative suggestions and some editing of my manuscript. I am also grateful to Monti Shalosky for her editing of the final rendition of this book previous to publication. It is indeed a pleasure to receive the support of so many for this humble project.

My life has been very blessed with loving family and friends for whom I am also most grateful. During my retirement, I have acquired a passion for pickleball that has brought many kind and wonderful friends into my life. You are too numerous to mention by name but if you know me, please trust that I am thankful to know you.

My most heartfelt gratitude goes to my Creator for my existence. This life has been very full, and I have deep joy and appreciation for it all. My years as a "spiritual vagabond" while in the cult were less than optimal but taught me much. From there, I was catapulted into learning about some of the psychological underpinnings of human existence and my own dysfunction. I feel inexorably blessed for the trajectory of my life. My time as a psychotherapist was such an honor and I remain humbled with the love, trust, and commitment my clients and I shared on our journey together.

My professional work led me to studying Bioenergetics and other somatically oriented psychological theories about how unprocessed emotions and trauma along with our unconscious false beliefs are manifested in the body. Interpersonal neurobiology further informed me about the brain and its mechanisms but could not explain the phenomenon of the "mind" until I delved deeply into the *Course in Miracles*. Transcribed by Helen Schucman, PhD, with the assistance of her colleague William Thetford, PhD the *Course* confirmed what quantum physics has discovered and more. Soon after the transcription was completed, Kenneth Wapnick, PhD became their associate and dedicated his life to teaching the *Course* material. His voluminous writings are a continued source of mentoring for me.

Acknowledgments

From these studies, I have learned that our mind is split between the unconscious, mindless part with all our ego defenses and false beliefs and the mindful or "right-mind." We are free to choose which we listen to, but a mindful choice gives access to our source of divinity, or the Holy Spirit. I have subsequently come to also appreciate and learn from the material Gary and Cindy Renard have presented through their books and podcasts on the *Course*.

The *Course's* teachings have become my foundation whose curriculum has helped me accept and understand so much about my life and the dynamics at play in this world. It has been instrumental in the resolution of the challenges I have narrated in this book. I feel blessed to have access to its love, truth, and wisdom.

"All the world's a stage, and all the men and women merely players…" Shakespeare wrote long ago. One could see life as a place of learning, the platform where our choices play out in our personal lives and globally, or we can choose to blindly pass through each day, engaging in the never-ending battles of fear, judgment, anger, guilt and their effects of sickness and suffering.

There are many paths in life from which we can choose. Thank you for allowing me the opportunity to share with you the one I have chosen, leading me to forgiveness, love, truth, and peace of mind.

About the Author

TARRA JUDSON STARIELL is a retired licensed marriage and family therapist (LMFT) who received a Master of Arts in Psychology from Chapman University. She additionally specialized in child and adolescent development. Needing to reclaim herself after twelve years in a cult, she returned to school and studied psychology to heal and subsequently help others.

For her recovery, she studied numerous modalities to address the trauma she had sustained. During this process, Tarra became certified as an EMDR II therapist and a Certified Bioenergetic Therapist (CBT) and Faculty Trainer. She has also been trained in Somatic Experiencing (SE). For her work with couples, she studied and utilized Emotionally Focused Couples Therapy (EFT).

While practicing, she was a Clinical Fellow of the American Association for Marriage, Family Therapists (AAMFT), a member of the California Association for Marriage and Family Therapists (CAMFT), and North County, California Marriage and Family Therapists (NC-CAMFT), and the International Institute for Bioenergetic Analysis (IIBA).

Tarra chronicled this journey in her first book, *Sanity Lost and Found: A True Story of Brainwashing and Recovery*. Using her life story as the backdrop she hoped to help others better their understanding of how childhood experiences impact us and how we become vulnerable to negative influences as a result. Included are ways to work through the resulting dysfunctional behaviors and patterns and what it takes to heal from the vicissitudes we all face in life. Most importantly, are the examples of the power of resiliency, compassion, and forgiveness.

Tarra's clinical work began with homeless, and substance abusing Vietnam veterans and continued with substance abusing, pregnant and/or parenting adolescents on probation. Besides providing therapy for these teenagers, she also presented groups on domestic violence, parenting skills, stress reduction and coping tools to eliminate substance abuse cravings. At another work location, Tarra provided counseling for adolescent boys in a gang-diversion program who were attending an alternative high school as part of their probation.

About the Author

Working with homeless and monolingual Hispanic families and their obese children, she joined other professionals offering changes in areas of behavioral health, nutrition, and lifestyle choices. Before moving to strictly private practice, she also did contract work with St. Clare's Homes and a grant-driven program awarded by Interfaith Community Services, the Robert Wood Johnson Foundation and Columbia University. As the therapist for this program named CASAWORKS, Tarra provided psychotherapy for homeless and substance-dependent women and their children on welfare. It was a pilot program researching welfare-to-work solutions.

In 2001, Tarra established the Center for SELF Discovery and also maintained an office in San Diego. She made a promise to her clients not to write about their experiences and instead is offering some of the lessons she has learned within these stories. *Flashpoints of Awareness* is a light summary of some personal experiences and pratfalls with their corrections; all shared in hopes of helping expand our awareness and sense of well-being.

www.ingramcontent.com/pod-product-compliance
Lightning Source LLC
Chambersburg PA
CBHW070437010526
44118CB00014B/2079